writing guides

ACTIVITIES

Fantasy STORIES

HILARY BRAUND & DEBORAH GIBBON

FICTION FOR AGES 5–7

CONTENTS

INTRODUCTION

The Scholastic *Writing Guides* series provides teachers with ideas and projects that promote a range of writing, bringing insights from educational research into the classroom. Each guide explores a different type of writing and provides example material, background information, photocopiable activities and teaching suggestions. Their aim is to enable teachers to guide the writing process, share planning ideas and develop themes as a context for writing activities.

The materials:
● motivate children with interesting activities
● break complex types of writing into manageable teaching units
● focus on and develop the typical features of particular types of writing
● provide original approaches to teaching.

Each book is divided into sections, beginning with examples of the type of writing being taught. These are followed by ideas for developing writing and projects that will extend over a series of sessions.

SECTION ONE: USING GOOD EXAMPLES

Section One looks at good examples of the genre, with the emphasis on using texts to stimulate and develop writing. Two example texts are shared, and questions that focus the discussion on their significant features are suggested. This is followed by activities that explore what the texts can teach us about writing, enabling teachers to compare the two texts and to go on to model the type of writing presented in the guide.

SECTION TWO: DEVELOPING WRITING

Section Two moves from reading to writing. This section provides activities that prompt and support children in planning and writing. A range of approaches includes planning templates and strategies to stimulate ideas. The activities refine children's ideas about the type of writing being developed and give them focused writing practice in the context of scaffolded tasks. Teacher's notes support each activity by explaining the objective and giving guidance on delivery.

SECTION THREE: WRITING

Section Three moves on to writing projects. Building upon the earlier work in Section Two, these projects aim to develop the quality of writing and provide a selection of ideas for class or group work on a particular theme or idea. The teacher may choose to use some or all of the ideas presented in each project as a way of weaving the strategies developed in Section Two into a more complex and extended writing task.

SECTION FOUR: REVIEW

Section Four supports the assessment process. Children are encouraged to reflect on the type of writing they are tackling and to evaluate how effectively their work has met the criteria for the genre identified in Section One.

Ace Dragon Ltd

John took the Underground to Dragonham East. There he saw a dragon in wellingtons.

The dragon said, "How do you do? I'm Ace Dragon Ltd."

John said, "How do you do? I'm John."

Ace and John found some waste ground and got ready to fight.

Ace said, "Best out of three?"

John said, "Right."

Ace and John had their first fight.

John won.

Ace and John had their second fight.

John won.

John said, "That's two in a row. That's best out of three. Now you have to take me flying."

John got on Ace's back and off they flew. Ace and John flew very high and very far.

John said to Ace, "Can you do stunts? Can you do sky-writing with fire?"

Ace did stunts and sky-writing with fire.

They were very high up and it was getting dark when Ace said, "I'm running out of petrol."

John said, "I didn't know you ran on petrol."

Ave said, "That's how I make my fire and that's what makes me go. I've used up so much petrol with the sky-writing that we haven't got enough to get us back."

John said, "Can't we glide back down to earth?"

Ace said, "No, we can't. If I stop flapping my wings we'll crash, and it's a very long way down."

John said, "Look! There's a little golden moon below us. Can you get that far?"

Ace said, "I'll try."

Russell Hoban

Daniel's Dinosaurs

Daniel loved dinosaurs. He loved big dinosaurs and he loved little dinosaurs.

At the library, he read books about dinosaurs. When he drew pictures, he drew pictures of dinosaurs. When he wrote stories, he wrote stories about dinosaurs.

Daniel's dinosaurs were everywhere. Two Plateosaurs lived next door. A Segnosaurus sat behind each check-out at the supermarket. An Allosaurus directed traffic, and one unknown variety barked at him from behind a high fence every morning as Daniel passed by on his way to school.

Daniel's teacher was a nice friendly plant-eating Diplodocus, but sometimes...

... she turned into a big fierce Tyrannosaurus.

Mary Carmine

SECTION ONE
USING GOOD EXAMPLES

From a very young age, children enjoy and appreciate fantasy stories. Their own imaginative play often makes use of fantasy to add excitement or to resolve problems, with characters suddenly becoming possessed of amazing powers or imaginary characters appearing to save the day. As they get older, children begin to introduce these features into their story writing. The activities in this book aim to help children to develop these ideas and to clarify the particular features of fantasy stories as distinct from, for example, fairy tales or scary stories.

The features to be identified and explored include the use of imaginary or imagined characters, fantasy worlds or settings, events which in real life are impossible or improbable, and the interaction between real and imaginary characters. The two text extracts on photocopiable pages 4 and 5 provide a starting point for investigating these features.

Shared activities

Ace Dragon Ltd
The extract on photocopiable page 4 tells of one little boy's encounter with a dragon and their adventures together, in the course of which they leave the original everyday setting and end up on a golden moon.

Discuss with the children the matter-of-fact tone of the writing. Rather than presenting John's encounter with the dragon as something amazing it appears to be perfectly normal to meet a dragon at an underground station and that the dragon should be wearing wellingtons. Talk about the aspects of the story that are rooted in real life and those that are purely fantasy.

Daniel's Dinosaurs
The second extract, on photocopiable page 5, shows how fantasy is rooted in one's imagination. Daniel's obsession with dinosaurs leads him to imagine that they are all around him in everyday situations. Draw attention to the Segnosaurus seated at the check-out in the picture. Focus on how in this story the characters stay in the real world and do not leave this everyday setting, in contrast to *Ace Dragon Ltd*.

Real life or fantasy?
Display an enlarged copy of photocopiable page 8. Talk about the illustrations of John and the dragon. Ask the children to tell you which character would be considered as real life and which as fantasy. Explain that you are going to work together to identify from the story extract of *Ace Dragon Ltd* features that are based on real life and those which are purely fantasy. Read through the headings 'Characters', 'Settings' and 'Events'. Ask the children to give you suggestions from the story extract which would fall into those categories and then decide as a class whether they should be recorded as real life or fantasy.

Jobs for the dinosaurs
Display an enlarged copy of photocopiable page 9. Ask the children if they know anything about the dinosaurs shown and discuss their characteristics, for example able to fly, has a long neck, very strong, fierce and so on. Explain that as in *Daniel's Dinosaurs* they are going to think of everyday jobs that they could imagine the dinosaurs doing. List these ideas in the box next to the relevant dinosaur. As a class, choose one of the ideas and work together to create a sentence reflecting the style of *Daniel's Dinosaurs*, for example *A pterodactyl flew past, delivering the post*. Repeat this for each of the dinosaurs shown.

writing guides: **FANTASY STORIES**

Taking ideas further

Through exploring the two text extracts on photocopiable pages 4 and 5, the children have had the opportunity to consider fantasy stories as a distinct genre and to begin to recognise the particular features of that genre. They have explored the difference between fantasy and reality and how these can be combined within the story. They have also looked at how fantasy characters may appear within a real-life setting or travel beyond this to imaginary places.

These two extracts provide a limited experience of fantasy stories so an additional class collection of appropriate books will provide valuable support to the children's work and ways of taking further the discussions about the main features of the genre. Books you might like to make available to the children include *But Martin!* by June Counsel (Corgi) in which an alien appears at school to a group of children; any of the *Dr Xargle* books by Jeanne Willis and Tony Ross (Red Fox) which tell of aliens' views of our world; *The Egg* by MP Robertson (Frances Lincoln), another tale of a boy's encounter with a dragon; *The Happy Rag* by Tony Ross (Andersen Press), two stories in one book telling of a boy and a girl's imagined games with their own 'happy rags'; *The Baby Who Wouldn't go to Bed* by Helen Cooper (Corgi) in which a baby converses with his toys which come to life as he tries to avoid bedtime; and *Out for the Count* by Kathryn Cave and Chris Riddell (Frances Lincoln), a counting adventure in which Tom meets a range of characters in his attempts to get to sleep.

You could work with the children to sort the book collection in various ways, facilitating further discussion about the features of fantasy stories. Examples of this could include asking the children to identify:

● stories which make use of fantasy characters such as monsters or aliens
● stories in which real-life characters take on fantastical characteristics, such as toys coming to life
● stories in which the fantasy characters are known only to one or two real-life characters
● stories which are set completely in a fantasy setting, such as on another planet or in an imaginary land.

The same or different?

The activity on photocopiable page 10 encourages the children to compare the two extracts from *Ace Dragon Ltd* and *Daniel's Dinosaurs*, and helps them to recognise that while fantasy stories may appear quite different there are also shared features that identify them as being of the same genre.

Explain to the children that the statements on the photocopiable sheet apply either to *Ace Dragon Ltd*, *Daniel's Dinosaurs* or to both. They should cut out the statements and place them in the appropriate boxes on the page. Read through the statements with the children before handing out copies of the sheet and asking them to complete the work independently.

Imagine that!

Photocopiable page 11 reminds the children how the particular features of fantasy stories come from the imagination and could not exist or happen in real life. The children's own original ideas can be added to the sheet and displayed to provide inspiration when they write their own stories.

Real life or fantasy?

Real life

Characters

Settings

Events

Fantasy

Characters

Settings

Events

writing guides: FANTASY STORIES

Jobs for the dinosaurs

What jobs might these dinosaurs be good at?

Pterodactyl	delivering post
Triceratops	digging up the road
Ankylosaurus	knocking down buildings
Brontosaurus	cleaning windows
Stegosaurus	cutting down trees

The same or different?

Put the statements in the right box.

Both stories

Daniel's Dinosaurs

Ace Dragon Ltd

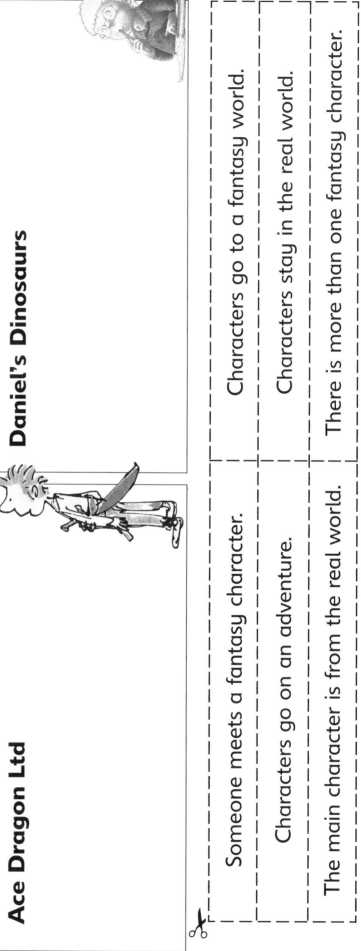

Someone meets a fantasy character.

Characters go on an adventure.

The main character is from the real world.

Characters go to a fantasy world.

Characters stay in the real world.

There is more than one fantasy character.

Imagine that!

Fantasy characters

Fantasy worlds

Improbable events

SECTION TWO

DEVELOPING WRITING

This section provides ideas for activities which will help the children explore in greater depth the main features of fantasy stories. The activities aim to help children develop ideas that can eventually be used to write their own original complete fantasy stories. The focus tends to be on the interplay between reality and fantasy, reflecting the content of the two text extracts explored in Section One. Some of the activities, however, allow the children to develop a story that is complete fantasy, with fantasy characters in a fantasy setting, for example by combining ideas developed in 'Fantasy worlds' and 'Fantasy characters' (pages 16 and 17).

The features of fantasy stories developed by the activities include:
- *beginnings and endings – encouraging the children to root the story in a real-life setting and to find a way to return to reality at the end*
- *fantasy characters – encouraging the development of original characters, and developing vocabulary to describe them*
- *improbable events – establishing a sequence of events and considering the difference between those which are possible and those which could only be fantasy*
- *interplay between fantasy and reality – encouraging children to place imaginary characters in real-life settings, or moving real-life characters to a fantasy world.*

The work resulting from these activities should be stored by the children for later use as they compose their own original stories.

Developing ideas

Provide the children with a wide range of examples of fantasy stories. The two text extracts used in Section One both centre around boys meeting or imagining easily identifiable fantasy characters (in this case a dragon and dinosaurs) in an everyday setting, so it is important to supplement these with a wider range of fantasy ideas. As already suggested, try to make a collection of books featuring fantasy stories with a range of characters and settings. You may also like to include complete copies of *Ace Dragon Ltd* (Red Fox) and *Daniel's Dinosaurs* (Scholastic), if possible, so the children can discover how the stories develop and are eventually brought to an end. Explore the book collection by looking specifically at the features examined in the photocopiable activities. Discuss the settings – does the story move from real life to a fantasy world? Is real life returned to at the end? Look at the fantasy characters – in which way are they purely fantasy, for example are they extinct, purely imagined, or have magic powers? Explore the relationship between the main characters – is the fantasy character visible to everyone? Are friendships formed? Discuss the way in which the story develops – how do we move from reality to fantasy? What is the sequence of improbable events? How is the story brought to an end?

Discuss with the children their own fantasies – imaginary places they would like to visit, improbable events they would like to experience, imaginary characters they would like to meet. Part of this discussion may focus on the difference between 'scary' scenarios and fantasies which are more enjoyable or adventurous. Emphasise that your work together on fantasy stories will be focusing on the latter.

It will also be beneficial to engage the children in shared-writing sessions to develop various ideas and themes to do with fantasy stories. These could range from brainstorming a list of fantasy characters, for example dragons, dinosaurs, aliens, monsters, to working together to create descriptive passages about characters or settings.

FANTASY WORLDS

WHAT YOU NEED

Photocopiable page 16, writing and drawing materials, board or flip chart.

WHAT TO DO

Brainstorm with the children a list of words that describe fantasy worlds. These can be fantasy worlds they have read about in story books or their own original ideas. Discuss the different words that they have thought of. Give out the photocopiable sheet of three different fantasy worlds. Taking each picture in turn, ask the children to describe what they see and to imagine who might live there. The children will come up with different ideas for the same world –use this as an opportunity to discuss how fantasy comes from our imagination. Ask them to add their characters to the pictures and describing words to the boxes below. The last box has been left blank for the children to create their own fantasy world.

OBJECTIVE
■ To describe fantasy-world settings.

FANTASY CHARACTERS

WHAT YOU NEED

Photocopiable page 17 copied onto card and cut into individual cards, paper, writing and drawing materials.

WHAT TO DO

Talk through the words on each of the cards with the children. Ask what types of words they are, using the word *adjective* if appropriate. Ask them, in turn, to pick a card and describe the fantasy character, including that particular adjective, to the rest of the group. (Silhouettes have been drawn so as not to limit the children's descriptions.) Go through the first card as an example with them first, if necessary. For example, *the Martian had* spotty *tentacles coming out of his head*. Encourage them to go further than simply stating *the Martian was spotty*, for example.

Now, ask the children to write a pen portrait of their own fantasy character. Ask them to include one of more of the words from the cards. You may want to do an example as a group first. The children can add their own adjectives and silhouettes to the three remaining cards to use within the class.

OBJECTIVE
■ To build up descriptions of fantasy characters using adjectives.

MAGIC POWERS

WHAT YOU NEED

Photocopiable page 18, writing and drawing materials.

WHAT TO DO

Ask the children to recall any stories they know in which the characters have magic powers. (For example, the little girl in *The Magic Finger* by Roald Dahl.) How were the characters' magic powers used in the stories? Discuss with the children magic powers they would like their characters to have and how they would use these powers. For example, what could happen in their story if a character had the ability to turn herself invisible? Ask the children to choose one of the characters illustrated on the photocopiable sheet (or they may wish to use all three) and imagine that the character is able to do something fantastic using their powers. They should write and draw their idea in the thought bubble(s) provided.

OBJECTIVE
■ To develop character profiles, describing fantasy characteristics.

OBJECTIVE
■ To use story settings from reading to begin to develop their own fantasy plots.

WHAT'S DOWN THERE?

WHAT YOU NEED

Photocopiable page 19, writing materials.

WHAT TO DO

Recall with the children the extract from *Ace Dragon Ltd* where John meets a dragon at an underground station and goes on an adventure with him. Explain how the underground station could be the start of many other adventures, not only with a dragon but with any other fantasy characters that may live down there. Talk through the headings on the photocopiable sheet and ask the children to fill in the boxes, thinking of different fantasy characters and the adventures they could go on. They may like to work collaboratively with each other, sharing their ideas, before completing the sheet.

OBJECTIVES
■ To develop a story line from a given starting point.
■ To move a story from reality into fantasy.

WHEN SUDDENLY...

WHAT YOU NEED

An enlarged copy of photocopiable page 20, writing and drawing materials.

WHAT TO DO

Using an enlarged copy of the photocopiable sheet, discuss with the children how a fantasy story often starts in reality before moving into fantasy. What appears to be normal can suddenly change with one sentence. Read through the story starter with the children, stopping at *when suddenly…* Ask the children to think of different ways to continue the sentence, changing the story into fantasy. (For example, *when suddenly… a huge, hairy monster jumped out in front of Kai, blocking his path*; *when suddenly… a bright green beam shone down from the sky and Callum disappeared*.) Write in their ideas for both sentences. If they wish, they can illustrate their scenes on the back of the sheet. Once completed, read through the story, drawing the children's attention to when and how the story moved from reality into fantasy.

OBJECTIVE
■ To develop a plot, using knowledge of fantasy-story features.

THE STORY GOES ON...

WHAT YOU NEED

Photocopiable page 21, writing materials.

WHAT TO DO

Read through the boxes on photocopiable page 21 with the children. Explain that the questions will act as prompts to help them develop their fantasy plots and take their stories further on. Taking each question in turn, ask the children to share their ideas before going on to answering them on the sheet individually. For children working collaboratively on ideas for a story, choose a scribe to write on an enlarged copy of the sheet.

COMING TO AN END

WHAT YOU NEED

An enlarged copy of the extract from *Ace Dragon Ltd* on photocopiable page 4, writing materials, board or flip chart.

WHAT TO DO

The previous two activities looked at how a fantasy story changes from reality into fantasy and how to develop the plot. This activity focuses on fantasy-story endings, when often the story changes back to reality. Read through the extract from *Ace Dragon Ltd* again with the children. Brainstorm ideas on what might happen next when John and Ace land on the little golden moon and on how to bring the story to an end. Act as scribe to write an ending to the story extract with the children, as a guided-writing activity.

Finally, tell the children that in the book, the story ends by John and Ace landing back safely in the real world and each going home for their supper. In what other ways do the children think the story could end back in reality?

OBJECTIVE
■ To predict fantasy-story endings.

SNAPSHOTS

WHAT YOU NEED

Photocopiable page 22, writing and drawing materials.

WHAT TO DO

This activity draws the last three activities together, looking at the structure of a fantasy story from beginning to end in a snapshot. Read through the boxes on the photocopiable sheet to the children and ask them to write or draw their ideas in the photo frames. Remind them of the previous activities and draw out the key elements that are included in a fantasy story. Enlarge the photocopiable sheet if the children are drawing rather than writing their ideas in the boxes.

OBJECTIVES
■ To identify key elements of plots in fantasy stories.
■ To write a story plan.

Fantasy worlds

Describe these fantasy worlds.
What characters might live there?

writing guides: **FANTASY STORIES**

Fantasy characters

spotty

hairy

friendly

beautiful

brave

tiny

slimy

gigantic

green

Magic powers

What magic powers could your characters have?
Write and draw about your ideas in the thought bubbles.

What's down there?

What's down there?	What's down there?
What happens next?	What happens next?
What happens after that?	What happens after that?

UNDERGROUND STATION

When suddenly...

It was the first day back at school after the Christmas holiday and Kai was looking forward to seeing his friends again. He had enjoyed Christmas with his mum and dad but was excited about meeting his friend at the end of the road.

As he hurried out of the door, he shouted bye and ran up the street. Kai could already see Callum waiting for him on the corner...

when suddenly... _____

_____

_____

_____

_____

Little did he know... _____

_____

_____

_____

It was turning out to be quite an extraordinary day!

writing guides: FANTASY STORIES

The story goes on...

To the end!

How do your characters feel?

What amazing thing happens?

Where do they go?

Do you have a real-life character?

Who is your fantasy character?

You are embarking on an adventure!

Snapshots

Reality
Can you think of a real setting for your story? Invent some real-life characters.

Fantasy
What is it that becomes unusual in your story? Does your story include fantasy characters?

Adventure
What amazing things happen to your main characters?

Reality
Do you end up where you began?

The children will now have accumulated a number of ideas, both through discussion and practical activities, which will provide a firm foundation on which to base their own original story writing. Before asking the children to embark on their writing, discuss the content and structure of their stories using the display pages in this section to guide and prompt them. Encourage the children also to refer back to their completed work from Section Two to inspire ideas.

The children's story writing will probably take more than one session, allowing them to move from the planning stage to the first draft to the final 'publication' of the finished story. This will depend on the age of the children or their confidence in writing. Children in the early stages of writing will find it easier to write the complete story in one go. Supplying a choice of presentation ideas such as ready-made books or paper with decorative borders will encourage neater presentation.

Story structure

This poster, on photocopiable pages 24 and 25, could be enlarged and displayed for the children. It reminds them of the key features of fantasy stories that they have identified in the course of their work in Section Two. Discuss the headings and the ideas displayed under each heading with the class and any extra ideas suggested by the children. Encourage them to keep referring to the poster as they write their own stories.

Fantasy land

The poster of an imaginary land on pages 26 and 27 can be enlarged and used with a group or the whole class. Alternatively, make copies for the children to work on individually or in pairs. The prompt questions are intended to stimulate the children's imagination. Encourage them to use the map in the planning stage of their story writing. They could answer the questions, add their own details to the map and change the character's name to suit their own ideas.

Wordbank

Enlarge the wordbank on pages 28 and 29 for the whole class to use. Talk through each heading with the children and invite them to read the example words listed. Ask them to suggest other words that may be useful, encouraging them particularly to think of 'interesting' vocabulary.

STORY STRUCTURE

Characters

a girl　　a boy

Fantasy

a dragon　　an ali

Settings

Real life

the street

your bedroom

the school playground

Fantasy worlds

another planet

underwater world

Journeys to fanta worlds

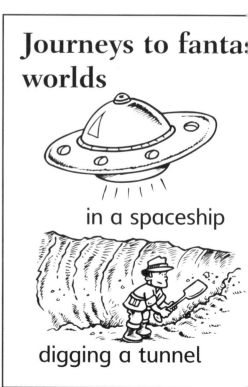

in a spaceship

digging a tunnel

Real life

a group of friends

a giant

Events

flying

a picnic

a dance

a toy coming to life

on a magic carpet

on a boat

Endings

back in bed

having your tea

walking home from school

FANTASY LAND

Who is flying across the sky?

Where does this path lead to?

What is in the forest?

writing guides: **FANTASY STORIES**

Who lives here?

How did Sam get here?

Where did this toy car come from?

Wordbank

Characters

Fantasy

alien
magic
extinct
gigantic
spotty

Real life

boy
girl
friend
teacher

Events

incredible
unbelievable
amazing

Journeys

whizzing
flying
spinning
suddenly

writing guides: FANTASY STORIES

Settings

Fantasy

planet
unusual
island

Real life

school
street
park
ordinary

Endings

home
bedroom
disappeared

SECTION FOUR
REVIEW

The photocopiable pages in this section provide guidance in assessing the children's writing of fantasy stories. The children are encouraged to assess their own work and to work as a group in assessing and appreciating each other's finished stories.

In addition to assessing the finished work in these ways you should also encourage the children to assess their work in progress. This can be done through individual conferences with the children, or by having group or class discussions in which attention is brought back to the display photocopiables from Sections One and Three, ensuring the children are using the key features of fantasy stories and incorporating a range of vocabulary.

What do you think?
Copy photocopiable page 31 onto card and cut along the lines to create nine individual question cards. Working with a group of children, invite them to take turns in reading their finished story to the group. The children listening should then take turns to pick a card and read out the question written on it. The author then replies to the question, giving their own assessment and evaluation of their work. You may like to encourage the rest of the group to add comments, reminding them of the importance of keeping their suggestions positive.

In the end
When the children have completed their writing they can use photocopiable page 32 to map out the content of their stories, ensuring all the key features were included. They may like to compare this to their earlier plans or storyboards to see how much their ideas have changed in the course of their writing.

writing guides: **FANTASY STORIES**

What do you think?

Describe your fantasy character.

What settings have you used in your story?

Why did you choose your fantasy character?

Would you change anything if you had to write it again?

What is your favourite part of your story?

Where did you get your idea from?

What interesting words did you use?

What was unusual about your story?

Where will your next fantasy story take you?

In the end

Real-life setting

The event

Real-life character

The journey

Fantasy character

Fantasy setting

writing guides: **FANTASY STORIES**